When Spring Comes

ROBERT MAASS

SCHOLASTIC INC.
New York Toronto London Auckland Sydney

For Hillary

ISBN 0-590-06864-4

Copyright © 1994 by Robert Maass.
All rights reserved. Published by Scholastic Inc., 555 Broadway, New York, NY 10012, by arrangement with Henry Holt and Company, Inc.

12 11 10 9 8 7 6 5 4 3 2 1   7 8 9/9 0 1 2/0

Printed in the U.S.A.   08

First Scholastic printing, March 1997

Spirits soar when spring comes.

A sweet fresh breeze blows.
Bright shades of green
decorate winter's bare trees.

Farmers plow or burn off
last year's stubble to get
the earth ready for planting.
Spring is the time to sow seeds
so there'll be crops
later in the year.

Rain and melting snow
make spring waters rush.
The season's warm days
and cool nights mean
maple sap can rise and
be tapped.

Crocuses peek their heads above the ground when spring comes.

Gardeners turn the soil so last year's bulbs will return to flower.

Animals big and small are born in springtime.
Foals nuzzle their dams.

A mother duck seems to say "make way for ducklings!"

After the long winter,
boats need sanding,
brick needs pointing,
and roofs need mending.

Fixing and cleaning,
tightening and airing

are spring tasks of repair and renewal.

When all the world turns
green and flowery again,

a blossom is enough
to inspire a painting.

Matzoh is part of
every Passover seder,
when families gather to
retell an ancient story.

Bonnets and bunnies
appear at Easter.
It's time
to hunt for eggs.

April showers
bring rain delays…

and May flowers.

When spring comes,
birds return from
winter homes and busily
build their nests
(as people curiously look on).

On May Day, there's dancing and Maypoles, music and sunshine.

It seems that all the world celebrates spring.

Tradition has it that spring is a time for love to blossom

and be affirmed.

As the season nears its end, and hot weather approaches,

we mark Memorial Day
to honor those who've fallen
for their country.

Spring makes us ready for the seasons to come. Roll on, summer!